Artful Approach

Dr. Vijay Anand Sriram V

BookLeaf Publishing

India | USA | UK

Presentation by *BookLeaf Publishing*

Cover Page Design by V.Vijay Krishna

Web: www.bookleafpub.com

E-mail: info@bookleafpub.com

ISBN:9789360947811

First edition 2024

Disclaimer

This compilation of poems on HR concepts is intended to offer insights and perspectives into various aspects of the HR domain. The author's goal is to positively influence readers' understanding and engagement with HR principles. However, it is important to note that the views expressed in these poems are solely those of the author and do not necessarily reflect official policies or procedures. Readers are encouraged to interpret the content in the context of their own organizational policies and regulations. Additionally, while the author endeavors to provide accurate and informative content, readers are advised to consult relevant authorities or professionals for specific guidance on HR-related matters.

DEDICATION

Dedicated

to

Positive Universal Consciousness

ACKNOWLEDGEMENT

"Gratitude is the music of the heart, and in composing the symphony of my journey, I find myself humbly acknowledging the myriad of influences that have shaped the pages of this poetry collection".

To the Almighty, the grand maestro orchestrating the universe, thank you for molding me into the storyteller I am today. Your divine guidance is my compass in this poetic odyssey.

To my pillars of strength—my father, mother, wife, and son—your unwavering support has been the foundation upon which my diverse expressions found their place in the world. To my extended family members, your encouragement echoed in the verses of every effort.

A heartfelt appreciation to the BookLeaf Publishing team for crafting a challenging yet invigorating 21-day, 21-poem quest. Your commitment to literary exploration has brought this collection to life.

I am deeply grateful to Mr. Sathiamoorthy, a dear friend, for referring me to Ms. Ambal Saravanan, a prominent HR Consultant. Her comprehensive review of my work, infused with her unique style, has been invaluable. Ambal's timely suggestions, ideas, and words of encouragement have elevated the Artful Approach to new heights, perfectly aligning it with the Corporate HR Circle. This book has truly become a must-read, thanks to her contributions.

To my circle of clients, friends, well-wishers, and professional associates, your continuous motivation has been the wind beneath my creative wings. In this collaborative dance, your rhythms have resonated in each poetic line.

A preemptive thanks to the readers—those adventurous souls who find solace, inspiration, or reflection in the written word. Your anticipation is the heartbeat that fuels my literary endeavors.

And to the vast cosmic network of kindred spirits who have vibrated with my essence, fostering growth and connection—your unseen influence is acknowledged with deep appreciation.

In this tapestry of gratitude, each thread represents a unique soul, and collectively, you've woven a narrative of support, inspiration, and growth. With heartfelt thanks, I extend my hand in acknowledgment.

Positive Universal Consciousness

Samastha Lokha Sukino Bhavanthu

PREFACE

ARTFUL APPROACH

Emotions   recollected   from   decades   of experience

Greetings Dear Readers,

In the intricate labyrinth of life, the quest for happiness often eludes us, a puzzle we earnestly try to solve. Many times, I grappled with this internalized question: What truly makes a person happy? A relentless search for achievements left me unsatisfied; the pursuit of money and wealth yielded no lasting joy; even in positions of power, happiness seems elusive. It was then that I stumbled upon a profound revelation – the transformative power of creative expressions and the unwavering commitment to giving my best in every endeavor.

This metamorphosis paved the way for my journey as a successful trainer, coach, filmmaker, author, and, most importantly, as a human being. As 2024 unfolded, I found myself yearning for another dose of happiness, and serendipity led me to "Artful Approach." Can poetry transcend its lyrical confines and become a potent training and coaching material? This universal question reverberated within me and became the genesis of this collection.

Written in a span of 21 days, each poem encapsulates not only the thoughts of the moment but draws from the well of experiences amassed over more than two decades. The verses within "Artful Approach" emerged as a revelation that poetry, with its rhythmic cadence, can indeed be a vehicle for transformative learning and personal growth.

One of the most captivating features of this book is its unique structure: each poem consists of precisely 21 lines, with word counts ingeniously adding up to combinations of 21 (e.g., 210, 201, 261, and 241). Moreover, the styles and themes of each poem vary, enriching the reader's experience with diversity and depth. In numerology, 21 holds special significance; number 2 represents harmony, balance, cooperation, and relationships, while number 1 signifies independence, individuality, and new beginnings. Together, they create a dynamic blend that embodies personal growth, creativity, and the pursuit of one's true path. I am confident that the "Artful Approach" will become a cherished treasure for a lifetime.

Inviting you all to ponder upon the question that birthed this collection. Can poetry be more than just words on paper? Can it be a guide, a mentor, and a companion in your quest for personal and professional excellence? I assure you that the time spent delving into the verses of "Artful Approach" will be one of the most productive and enriching phases of your life.

This collection is not merely a set of poems; it's a journey into the realms of introspection, motivation, and leadership wisdom. As you traverse through these pages, may you witness a rebirth—a new you emerging, enriched with happiness, peace, joy, and the abundance of wealth that transcends material realms.

Believe in the transformative power of poetry, believe in the potential within you, and let "Artful Approach" be your guide on this remarkable journey.

Let happiness, peace, joy and wealth be your blessing every second.

Reader's Reflections on "Artful Approach"

"An extremely powerful message on the HR concepts depicted in a poetry format, truth and humour integrated in the right amount. HR is the gate to hell or heaven depending on the work you are placed at. The different roles of HR and its impact on the employee are well versed. Give it a try folks, it sure is going to make you smile and make you hit or hug your HR. It is both entertaining and educational."
-Deepa Balachandran
Project Coordinator,
Ministry of Health,
United Arab Emirates.

"A unique effort by Vijay Anand Sriram to navigate the corporate realm in an artistic way. The Artful Approach presents Corporate HR concepts in a simple and poetic manner that captures the minds of HR professionals, leaders, and employees, spreading a positive wave. I appreciate the author for his uniqueness, positivity, and purpose in creating this distinctive work."
-Vijayabharathi
Senior Delivery Manager,
Global ER&D Services,
L&T Technology Services Ltd,
India.

"Dr. Vijay has skillfully navigated HR concepts from recruitment to the future of HR in an astonishing manner. His approach, emphasizing the importance of understanding HR concepts in an artful way, is truly the need of the hour. I have a particular fondness for his take on PoSH; I am confident that you will all cherish this poem. Congratulations, Vijay, on a remarkably professional and captivating piece of work."

-Sathiamoorthy Narayanan
Head- Engineering and Capital Markets
Intellect Design Arena Limited,
India.

"The Life Skills-based HR Approach, functioning as a ladder to bridge the generation gap, is a pivotal step towards corporate success. Emphasizing "we" over "I" in the corporate grammar sets the tone for a harmonious journey. Dr. Vijay's work, reminiscent of the thunderous rain, inundates us with a plethora of profound thoughts. This natural blend of HR processes is bound to inspire and motivate the younger generation. Wishing Dr. Vijay all the best on this powerful endeavor."

-Saravanan Palanivelu
Vice President,
Eversendai,
India.

"Dr. Vijay's Artful Approach is a simple yet potent tool for mastering HR concepts. With two decades in the service industry, I truly appreciate how he seamlessly integrates art into management. His emphasis on empathy, creativity, and the concepts of unlearning, relearning, and learning are indispensable skills for achieving corporate success in the future. This book is a must-read and a treasure trove for every aspiring professional aiming for career success."

-Dr. K. Lakshmi
Managing Director,
RIPE Consulting,
India.

1

Artistic Application

Covering Letter for Job Application

Amidst this technologically advanced world of
hardware,
You have an emotionally competent superhuman
software.
Hiring me will lead to a world of 10X greater
productivity,
Avoiding me will lead you to search in a pool of
resource paucity.
My degree has prepared me as a field expert,
To manage my job responsibilities with greater
adept
Moving with my colleagues is the easiest of all,
Because I am a very strong team player after all
I am not looking at this offer as a mere job,
My focus is to build a strong career others
cannot rob.
Learning, unlearning, and relearning will be my
regular routine,
Lethargy, unfair practices, and revolt behavior I
will not entertain.
My eye for detail is absolutely magnetic,

The results you get because of this will be
fantastic.
Innovative self-starter is my habit,
Big initiatives with greater results for the
organization, I will grab it.
Offer me this wonderful position,
Watch the magic of the organization growing
with greater reputation.
When I am at the office, every day is fun,
positivity, laughter, and happy moments,
Waiting for the offer letter to create magic
moments
In this new role, I'll be the catalyst for sure
success transformative accomplishments.

2

Induction Catalyst

Induction Program Strategies

The debate was about what to say and what not,
Managers focused on employees' monetary
rebates, a thought.
One courageous manager asked,
If money alone is the requirement, why even do
this task?
Everyone was silent, and they all knew
Money alone cannot make the difference, it's
true.
The quality of life at the office will be a strong
point of reference,
Everyone comes to work with a goal; no doubt,
they work with diligence.
Creating a winner requires a lot of thought on
HR Policy rework,
Including empathy and creativity as pillars to
ensure trust at work.
Thus, every employee works with passion on the
job entrusted,
Empowering these resources will be the motto of
the organization we trust.

Enlightened, they will feel their work without
any draining,
By guiding every employee, managers should
become mentors grading.
Under mentors' guidance, employees become
ambassadors as soon as they enter,
Never allow gossip, back-biting, fault-finding,
and complaints at the office to center.
Remember, an organization with values will be
adored for its service,
Business with purpose should be driven at an
early stage during induction, a practice.
To ensure avoiding all kinds of conflict
resolution,
Motivating the team continuously in one form or
another is the key, an obligation.
You will find the magic of motivation when
employees work like busy bees.

3

Professional Wedding

Optimizing Recruitment - Tips & Tricks

In dreams, we seek a lifelong voyage with a
beautiful stunning partner,
Yet, a corporate companion emerges, chosen
without our whisper.
Multiple profiles dance in the pursuit of one
description,
HR's pride in filtering, a ballet of qualified
"prescription".
Qualification, physique, wealth, health, and
attitude, the criteria cast,
In the corporate ballet, emotional maturity,
knowledge, skills, charisma, will be the perfect
blast.
One-on-one, the final act, sealing the alliance
with grace,
As in job interviews, technical rounds and HR's
embrace.
Understanding the inner view, vital for marital
delight,
Corporate weddings echo interviews, revealing
insight.

Equality, empowerment, mutual care, the
modern marriage pledge,
In the corporate sphere, mentors, colleagues, a
supportive edge.
Prior understanding and mutual acceptance, a
key to marital bliss,
Quality Knowledge transfer, positive motivation,
a manager's talent, ensuring work's gentle kiss.
No authority, anger, defaming and comparison,
in love's name,
Madness it is, to pressure, gossip, disrespect and
scold, seeking corporate fame.
Day by day, in every way, relationships must
grow,
Motivation's daily chorus makes a team's
performance glow.
Trust and love, the foundation of familial grace,
In careers, empowerment, and faith, a
timely-paced race,
Corporate wedding, a union of terms and
conditions, a poetic embrace, redefining
matrimonial renditions.

4

Respectex

PoSH Awareness

In a daze, a group perplexed, faces with
confusion arrayed,
Their minds entangled, thoughts infused, in a
chaotic cascade.
A discussion arose, the focal theme PoSH
Awareness Training,
Understanding dawned, confusion unveiled,
purposeful meaning gaining.
What's wrong in a workplace bond? a voice, a
fervent noise,
Nothing, if professional, I replied, aiming to
hush the voice.
How to foster professionalism in a lifestyle open
and free?
Know your limits, hold values clear, and let
them define thee.
Touching, hugging, partying, and traveling, are
these crimes?
Caring touch, brotherly hug, celebration, and
travel, perfectly primes.
Love at first sight, love unbounded, love is
blind, they pled,

When trust, care, and respect abound,
colleagues' love is spread.
Dress, behavior, signs, advances, concerns that
persist,
Treat as kin, brothers, ensure advances desist.
In the realm of PoSH, questions unravel,
answers weave,
A poetic discourse, awareness unfurls, like
leaves on a breeze.
Boundaries known, relationships professional, a
harmonious theme,
A workplace ballet, where respect and care
gleam.
With understanding and friendship, let
workplace bonds be,
A symphony of professionalism, in unity and
glee.
In this awareness tapestry, threads of wisdom
intertwine,
A lesson in PoSH, where boundaries align.
So let awareness bloom, like flowers in spring,
in the garden of respect, let professionalism sing.

5

Mission Marvel

5 W and 1 H Career Success Keys

Will a brief interview decide my ability?
To work with sincerity, achieving maximum
productivity?
Stuck on day one, awaiting answers,
HR Manager provided a practical solution,
easing my anger.
Recruiting starts with analysis, the department's
foundation we weave, she said.
Attitude, qualifications, and skills create the
requirement thread, I perceived.
Universal is the requirement, a playful tease I
wanted to lead.
Every organization has a vision, mission,
objectives, she asserted, made me feel rugged,
indeed.
Based on the above, she explained, organization
shapes its goals, she claimed.
Turning inward, understanding nuances, in her
view, I aimed.
A good process and plan, trouble-free, resources
aligned.

An idea to explain the hiring process, a bundle, she outlined.
When do you need a candidate?" she inquired, thought shared.
"If 10X revenue earned, hiring justified," math declared.
"Brilliant," she praised, into the next puzzle, she dared.
"Why hire a resource?" a question in the air.
"Hiring for value addition, no hustle," I declared.
"Interesting," she pondered, "Who should be hired?"
"Simple," I replied, "Positive attitude, skills acquired."
"Where can I locate you?" she asked, my answer inspired.
In a team with energy, empowerment is required.
"What you do really matters; how you do it can create wonders."

6

Dhoni Army

Winning & Energetic Team Building Strategies

One project two teams on the project was the
challenge
Literally all were confused and felt crazy about
Management's strange idea
Qualities of winning team was the first exercise
we started to focus and prepare
Don't reinvent the wheel I said let us first do an
internal repair
All the members felt offended with my
statement,
I realized that only action-oriented solutions will
become testament
My first question to my team was Dhoni or
Sachin who is the best?
Sachin is the greatest of all cricketing legends
Dhoni is the coolest captain king
Team adored Dhoni for his ability to lead the
individuals
For a successful team it's not Me, it's WE the
winner manual
What are WE a sarcastic voice propped up for
getting clarity

Appreciate, apologize and be accountable is WE chariot with sanctity

Winning strategies for WE Team, I elaborated to ensure meaningful collaboration

Setting SMART Goals, Thinking before implementing, focused action

The three important foundations after team formation

Appreciating differences, empathetic communication, and data-based decision

Most important skills for successful team transformation

Consistency, shared values and mutual respect

The key propellers for the team to travel a long journey with impact

WE teams can create winning organization

7

Bloodless Fight

Conflict Resolution Strategies

In times of discord, disagreements, and
frustration, speak with grace,
Choosing moments for alignment, hearts finding
the right space,
Plan with focus, care, and empathy,
understanding's seed sown,
No blame, no shame, no names, let kindness
lead, a path known.
Give information with clarity, truth unveiling its
tale,
A saga of positive resolution, where respect sets
sail.
Listen keenly and attentively, with an open
heart,
Show understanding, and real concern, a crucial
part.
Talk it through with melody, a dance of
conversation,
No threat of violence or harm, just a chance for
restoration.
Choose a good time to speak with openness,
when spirits align,

Plan well in advance the script with kindness, let harmony shine.
No blame game, no specific name-call, qualification and status keep it light,
Give and take, accept, apologize and appreciate, finding common sight.
Listen deeply, to words and body language unspoken,
Show you're absolutely present, mending the bonds that were broken.
Talk it all through, let the conflicts unfold,
In the language of peace and harmony, stories retold.
A gentle resolution, in words and action, we find,
In the conflict's realm, hearts realigned.
Arise, awake, and stop not till conflicts resolve, in the symphony of understanding, problems dissolve.

8

Mind Guard

Psychological Safety Strategies

In realms where minds entwine, warmth begins
to glow.
Psychological haven, where hearts trust beats
gently flow.
Curiosity triumphs with unique flavor, blame
takes a humble bow,
Learning predominates over shame, innovation's
a plenty seed we sow.
Organizational echo with valor, resilience firmly
begins to soar,
Competence prevails everywhere, a workforce
we always adore.
In the safety of dissent, respectful and
meaningful debates bloom,
Creativity celebrates, dispelling shadows of
gloom.
Inclusion safety, true selves embraced with
maximum pride,
Learner's ultimate sanctuary, where questions
gracefully abide,
Contributor's crafted shelter; voices smoothly
blend in a harmonious choir,

Challenger's chosen refuge, candor sparkles in their fire.
A melody of joyful safety, a learning problem we confess,
Fallibility acknowledged, curiosity our finesse.
Questions, arguments, discussions dance freely, like beautiful whispers in the breeze,
Rules set in stone, where employee engagement finds ease.
Conflict embraced, innovation, creativity, risks find their rightful rhyme,
Negativity reframed a journey of learning, unlearning and relearning all the time.
Open spaces for dialogue, discussions, presentations and arguments- an impactful communication's gentle grace,
Consistent measures, quality improvement, long-term bonding tracing paths of long-term embrace.
Consider the context, wisdom weaving through the air, a poem of safety, a guide to navigate with care.

9

Homework

Work from Home Strategies

In the office's dance, sweet vibes, laughter,
coffee breaks—a melody hums.
COVID-19 struck, home turned into an
unforeseen work conundrum.
Sweatpants adaptation, a desk by the kitchen's
informal nook,
Home, once a personal space, now entangled in
the professional outlook.
Dopamine dreams completely shattered,
oxytocin takes a comedic hit,
Zoom calls in loungewear, formal attire feels
like a perfect misfit.
Dedicated workspace, a desk by the bathroom's
quirky door,
Living room's off-limits, no spreadsheets
staining the floor.
Real WFH hours, not a never-ending digital
work spree,
Goals and priorities set, my to-do list is the
decree.
Time apps juggle minutes, as the clock sneaks a
clever sly,

Brief breaks for survival, sanity to hilariously
glorify.
Exercise intervals, stretch like a
work-from-home comedy show,
Music in the background, the rhythm helps me
comically flow.
From the office kingdom to the home-bound
comedic strife,
In this wild blend, navigating my amusing
work-life,
Loungewear-clad warrior, in this virtual realm I
amusingly comb,
Virtual calls, knowledge transfer and deadlines,
in my living room, I whimsically roam.
Through struggles and laughter, in this
work-home jest,
Adapted to this lifestyle and decided to give my
best,
WFH escapades, a 21-line popular comical
quest, based on reader's request.

10

LINKINSTA

Social Media Deaddiction Strategies

Social media whispers in the digital rhythm, our daily enhancer.
Two hours, twenty-seven minutes daily, a virtual connection destruction enhancer.
Eight years of scrolling, an online journey enhancer,
Yet family conversations lost a true-life imbalance enhancer.
Brains buzzing with likes, comments, reposts a constant enhancer,
Yet workplace talk slipping, lost in the digital trance enhancer.
Obsessed with the feed, forgetting real-life circumstance enhancer,
A boon of connection or a bane of digital expanse enhancer,
Tips for control, learn from top brands, a wisdom enhancer,
Consistent, quality posts, avoiding the overposter syndrome enhancer.
Your social media voice, be trendy, a smooth enhancer,

Overselling, overposting, curiosity, a digital
imbalance enhancer
Check your analytics, insights, and expert
recommendations; don't be a clueless enhancer,
Deleting negativity, unwanted comments, posts a
wise, strategic enhancer.
Beneath the digital sky, be a superior guide, not
a chance enhancer.
In any situation, don't let social media be your
quality of life enhancer,
A partner to interact, not a judge, nor an
evaluator enhancer,
A funny twist to virtual life, a humor creator
enhancer,
Yet amidst the chaos, laughter is the ultimate
enhancer,
A digital comedy break, a mood-lifting
enhancer,
Don't let screens rule, rule your screens, be the
enhancer.

11

Chronicles of Yes or No

Art of Saying NO

In the quality of tasks, your talent shines, a
resounding yes,
A daunting task, your competence drains and
you fail a confident no
In the glow of eagerness, work is interesting and
within your time limit, a resounding yes
Over time, burnout, high stress, no personal
priorities, a confident no
Your silence makes them take it all, sparing you,
a resounding yes
Reflect, recognize, in your zeal and you feel
tempted to work more, a confident no
Value your time, let commitments in priority
flow, a resounding yes
A heartless manager, a ruthless colleague's
attractive offer, confident no
Steps towards self-care, growth, discipline and
evaluation, a resounding yes
Stop being overly nice, let boundaries boldly
show, a step towards a confident no.
Preempt the flood, let proactive no's start to
grow, a resounding yes

Pleasing others, overworking, burning out, and
losing peace, a confident No
In the language of powerful no, finding the
power of your soul, a resounding yes
Being a victim, in control of others, and losing
self-respect, a confident no
Thinking twice, working out the permutations
before saying NO, a resounding yes
Impulsive yes, slogging like a bull, all the time
work and work, a confident no
Empowering your choices, situational
assertiveness, smiling at work, a resounding yes
Spoiling your health, peace, losing harmony in
family because of overwork, a confident no
Taking time to say no, sticking on to your
decision, a resounding yes
Getting wedded to your job, incentives and the
company, a confident no
Yes or No, the decision to rejoice is in your
hands.

12

EXEN

Diversity and Inclusion Strategies

At fifty, my boss's years gracefully engage in
life's dance,
Half that, I navigate, on the youthful stage,
taking a chance.
Discipline, his anthem, echoes through the
corridors of time,
In the realm of deadlines, my success
continuously chimes.
A relic of a phone outdated, vintage, firmly held
in his experienced grasp,
Mine futuristic, advanced and attractive a tale
yet to fully grasp.
Gen X meets Z, thoughts collide in workplace
vibrant hues,
Criticism of any kind repels him, while
constructive criticism my growth it strews.
Work first, client first, family trails, a path less
trodden,
Deadlines matter, family, seeds I've sown.
A gap may seem apparent in many ways, but
bridges we can weave,
With a plan in seven steps, let's together believe.

Open minds and empathy, a know-it-all we
consciously shun,
Transparency in communication, expectations
spun.
Respect for his age, my energy a pact warmly
embraced,
Wisdom and agility's synergy, a harmonious
chase
Situations and problems, not faces become our
guide,
Life skills blend with tech, a shared design
worldwide.
Hangouts unite, victories celebrated with a toast,
Personal space sacred, no invasions engrossed.
Humor and depth, a poetic decree, in this gap of
generations, a bridge, let it be.

13

The 36th Chamber of Shaolin

Importance of Training and Coaching

Training and coaching, vital for success's flight,
guidance and expertise, illuminating our
professional light.
A foundation laid, from the career's dawn,
instills determination, for achievement to spawn.
Coaching, a potter with the clay of our fate,
directs us right, on the path that is great.
Polished and refined, we shine bright, skills and
expertise, our armor, our might.
Confidence built, through training's embrace,
gracefully we excel, winning the challenging
race.
It's not just learning, but growth profound, an
oath against giving up, in challenges we're
bound.
From speaking to leadership's peak, conquering
fears, new thrills we seek.
Training transforms weakness into strength,
redefining abilities, at any length.
Time management skills, a cure for
procrastination, defending goals, a clear path to
our destination,

Strategic plans expand, potential unbound, breaking free from limitations, in victory we're found.

Confidence in abilities, a limitless sea, opening possibilities, setting our potential free

Coaches and trainers, a heartfelt gratitude we share, for guiding our journey, with utmost care.

Embracing training and coaching, keys to success, and hard work, goals we impress.

Thanks to training, coaching's gentle touch, our future, a lesson in wisdom, a journey we clutch.

Success draws near, with knowledge as our guide, skills as our gear, in career's stride.

Unbridled and clear, our story unfolds, in training and coaching, our destiny molds.

Guidance shapes paths, coaching's art reveals ways forward.

Learning's embrace, career's tapestry woven with wisdom threads

Mentors illuminate, knowledge propels, and success's journey unfolds brightly.

Resilience blooms, challenges met, triumphs etched in resilience.

Embrace transformation, training's gift, a journey of continuous growth.

14

Review Rhythm

Strategies for Superior Performance Appraisal

Managers, it's time to learn, about performance
appraisals, a crucial concern,
For career growth and a quality life, this process
can make or break, all the organizational hype.
There are seven key elements, you must know,
to conduct a good appraisal,
Get feedback on your review process, make it a
regular habit, and don't let it regress.
Have frequent, less formal chats, about the
appraisal; don't let it fall flat,
Come rehearsed and make time for each review,
giving the attention they're due.
Train yourself on active listening, it's important,
there's no dismissing,
Give specific feedback that is actionable; sure
it'll motivate and boost performance,
unquestionable.
During the review, make plans for the future, set
clear goals, for them to grow and nurture,
Offer support and opportunities for growth, this
will be appreciated by both.

Conducting a successful review, preparation is
the key, make sure you do,
Set clear goals and encourage self-evaluation,
this will foster improvement, no hesitation.
Give constructive feedback, in a kind tone; make
it a two-way conversation zone,
Regular check-ins, keep the communication
alive, document everything, so nothing's left to
strive.
Follow up on feedback, see it through, this will
show your employees, that you value,
Their hard work and dedication, it's the key to a
successful organization.
So managers, it's time to take charge, an
appraisal can make or break, don't let it barge,
Be a mentor, coach and leader to your team, they
will do wonders like a sunbeam
"Remember, you have passed through this stage
once; it's a very hot seat, that can crunch"
Everyone knows proof is in the pudding,
remember to be smooth after all they are
budding
Inspirational and motivating, be your tone; let's
make corporate life, a perfect happy zone.

15

Skill Peak

Importance of Upskilling and Reskilling

Upskilling and Reskilling the team, a vital part
of organizational gleam
The world keeps changing, that's no lie,
technology and trends keep flying by
Hybrid work models, new corporate culture,
calls for employees to grow and nurture
For organizations to reach new heights, their
workforce must be trained in new sights
From doers to decision makers, the team must
become great thinkers
The power of AI has brought the need, for skills
to evolve with lightning speed
Gone are the days of mundane tasks, now soft
skills and hard skills are asked
Managers, listen and make a plan, to help your
team become the best they can
Set clear goals and make them see, the need for
upskilling to succeed
Blended learning, a convenient way, to learn and
grow in today's workday
Be a mentor, lead by example, chase your
dreams, and let them be ample

Hold your team, guide them right, and watch
them progress, with all their might
Make the process fun and exciting, by investing
in skills that are enlightening
Soft skills to communicate and connect, hard
skills to excel and perfect
Embrace this new corporate life, by evolving
and growing in this world of strife
For when we learn, we reach new heights, and
organizations thrive, as we unite
Never settle down for less, skilling can make
you glow perfect
Remember to sharpen the axe before ever cut to
make the job perfect
Some may learn, some may not, as a manager
your duty is to train them a lot
Upskilling and reskilling the team, a journey that
may seem like a dream
But with hard work and dedication, we can make
it a reality, with determination

16

THINK TO INK

Importance of Thinking Skills

In the fast-moving corporate life, creativity is
the key to thrive.
It breaks the rules and sets us free, to turn ideas
into a winning spree.
With every problem, there's certainly a new way
to see the world.
Finding patterns in the unknown, connecting
dots all on our own.
Innovative thinking is easy, with an unstructured
process like a brainstorming exercise.
Or approach it with a structured mind, use lateral
thinking to find.
To improve creativity, we must pause; build
inspirational rituals without a cause.
Create something each and every day, let ideas
bloom and sway.
Instead of discipline, let's think of devotion,
watch our minds open like an ocean.
Find inspiration in our surroundings, amazing
ideas from simple things.
Make a list, pick the best, for our thoughts are
truly blessed.

Think outside the box, with every idea, break
new locks.
Have fun with colleagues and friends, in the end,
it's the journey that never ends.
Work during your most productive hours, see
creativity blossom like flowers.
In the world of corporate life, creativity is more
than just a skill.
It's a tool that helps us thrive; our passion for it
will always strive.
Creativity's magic, a spark in the corporate
dance,
An endless journey, where innovation finds its
chance,
Unleash imagination's fire, let it spread and
inspire.
In the canvas of ideas, paint a picture that won't
tire.
Forge a path of innovation, let creativity make
you a live wire

17

COMMUNICATION MARATHON

An Impact Communication

Authority in the realm, words hold sway.
Negotiation dances, forging bonds in the fray.
Interesting tales weave a tapestry grand,
Morale blossoms in this poetic land.
Passionate verses paint emotions bold,
Assertive cadence, a tale to be told.
Clear and Free in the canvas of communication,
Trustworthiness makes the mood sail in
meditation.
Concise messages, succinct and pure,
Objective discourse, a foundation secure,
Meticulous crafting, each word refined,
Meaningful dialogue, a rare kind,
Unique, a style, to keep in mind,
Nurturing tones, a perfect knight,
Innovative thoughts, a spark in the night,
Complete narratives, woven tight.
Artistic vision, words painted on air,
Time bound a commitment to bear.
Inquisitive questions take flight,
Optimistic echoes, dispelling the night,
Noble intention, achieve excellence.

18

Engage to Enlighten

Importance of Employee Engagement Activities

In offices where work can be a little cloudy, boring and bland,
Engagement and fun make the place truly grand.
Mentors can guide with a smile, hope, care and friendly hand,
Every work becomes a circus, a creative band.
Managers should have visions, like a flowing stream,
Then Energetic employees can turn projects into a dream.
Employee Engagement's need and importance, let's all totally agree,
Brings joy, laughter and productivity, as happy as can be.
Breaks, outings, treats and games, lifting the mood so good,
Creating a culture, cheerful and full of positive mood.
Senior Mentors, be the guiding light, so that organisation can shine bright,

Surely can push the employees to strive, with all
their might.
Forward-thinking top level management, a true
treasure chest,
With a sense of purpose and mission, we are
truly blessed.
Their support and leadership, we truly admire,
Guiding us through challenges, trouble and
setting us on fire.
In this complex world of corporate where
employees work like a bee hive,
Fun, games, rewards and engagement make
work a joyful dive.
With management, mentors, managers, and
employees in grace,
Sustaining, Thriving, growing, and laughing, in
this happy space.
Raise a toast to this workplace so fine.

19

Lead through Action

An Invitation to Achieve Excellence

Leadership's rarity shines, a quality cherished by the chosen few.
Guiding ships through turbulent storms, it's a skill beyond measure and view.
Excellence at its core empowers all those within the circle,
Every step, implore for greatness, a relentless miracle.
Empathy, a vital tool, fosters understanding and genuine care,
Creating a powerful rule, a team beyond compare.
Enrichment, a grand goal, nurtures growth in every endeavor,
Every task, a chance to sow seeds that flourish forever.
Envisioning the future through turns of time, a leader's guide,
In each vision, a lesson learned, in challenges, they abide.
Enlightenment, the key to inspire, and guide,

Every move, a set free, ignites a strong passion
worldwide.
Enablement, a feat crucial, granting the team a
chance,
To rise, to shine, seizing opportunities in the
dance.
Engineering skills, a rare gift, building and
planning with grace,
Every project, a daring venture, paves ways for
progress to trace.
Excellence, the ultimate goal, a leader's guiding
star,
Achieving it requires sharing the best, near and
far.
In the corporate world's hustle, where each day
is a climb,
Leadership's excellence paves success, an
enduring paradigm.
A skill, a talent, a coveted gift, Strive to achieve,
let your goals uplift.

20

Just for Laughs

A compilation of diverse thoughts gathered cohesively in one instance

We sit tight in our cubicles, every single day,
Staring at computer screens, in a monotonous way,
But don't be fooled, we're not just clones,
We have personalities, think and try to move on.
We attend meetings, with PowerPoints galore,
Nodding our heads for every slide, but never sure,
What's really going on, in this business world, don't stay outdated,
Start learning, keep growing and be updated.
Our language is full of buzzwords and cliches,
From 'thinking outside the box', to 'let's circle back, okay?',
We throw them around, like confetti in the air,
Hoping to impress, with our corporate affair
But amidst the chaos, there's something we've found,
A camaraderie, that brings us all around,
We may be totally stressed, but we're in this together,

And that's what makes us a great corporate
ensemble.
So here's to the corporate life, full of twists and
turns,
But we'll keep on pushing until, our success
flames,
And when we look back, at this time in our
lives,
We'll remember all the laughter, fun, joy and the
friendships we've flourished.
So let's keep on working and working, in this
corporate world,
With our puns and jokes, and our minds with
complete positivity unfurled.

21

Competence Map to Technological Triumph

A Foreteller of Future Workplace

In the nexus of technology and HR competence,
unfolds a double-edged sword,
As rapid streams of innovation surge, humanity
strives to hold its accord.
Yet, competence lags behind, a challenge yet to
be consoled,
Abuse of brilliance takes the main stage,
pleasure's pursuit extolled.
Shortcuts, laziness, procrastination and
backdoors weave a momentary wage,
Technology's transient din engages its benefits
on every page.
Corporate life mirrors this ever-shifting cage,
Unemployment rises, competence falters, and
attrition seeks to disengage.
Warnings from AI and ML echo, the workforce
wary of the decree,
Revolt against learning and adopting tech skills
forms a formidable plea.

In the face of challenges and adversities,
wisdom holds the key,
For employees, continuous striving, learning
technology's insights where opportunities thrive.
From typewriters to keyboards, changes live,
Apply technology wisely, purpose in every
drive.
Continuous improvement, elevate to manage the
tide,
View technology not as a permanent guide.
A tool to refine work, where excellence abides,
In this dynamic realm, innovation and creativity
reside.
Organizations embrace the power of technology,
data as guides, ensuring proper methodology.
Train the workforce, incentivize and reward
those shaping the legacy.
For the future of corporate life, a path clear,
navigate with wisdom, let innovation steer.

GLOSSARY OF TERMS

A

1. AI:

AI, or Artificial Intelligence, refers to the simulation of human intelligence processes by machines, typically computer systems. These processes include learning (the acquisition of information and rules for using the information), reasoning (using rules to reach approximate or definite conclusions), and self-correction. AI systems are designed to perform tasks that would typically require human intelligence, such as visual perception, speech recognition, decision-making, and language translation. AI technologies include machine learning, natural language processing, computer vision, robotics, and more, and they are increasingly used across various industries to automate processes, enhance productivity, and solve complex problems.

B

2. Blended Learning:

Blended learning is an educational approach that combines traditional face-to-face instruction with online learning activities. It integrates various delivery methods, such as classroom lectures, hands-on workshops, virtual discussions, and digital resources, to create a flexible and interactive learning experience. Blended learning allows learners to engage with course materials both in-person and remotely, providing opportunities for self-paced study, collaborative learning, and personalized feedback. By leveraging technology alongside traditional teaching methods, blended learning aims to enhance learning outcomes, increase learner engagement, and accommodate diverse learning styles and preferences.

3. Blame Game:

The "Blame Game" refers to a situation where individuals or groups attempt to shift responsibility or accountability for problems, mistakes, or failures onto others rather than taking ownership themselves. It often involves pointing fingers, making accusations, and deflecting criticism in order to avoid personal or organizational consequences. This behavior can hinder effective communication, damage relationships, and impede problem-solving efforts, ultimately undermining productivity and morale within a team or organization.

C

4. Covering Letter:

A cover letter introduces you to an employer, complements your resume and explains why you are a good fit.

5. Catalyst:

A catalyst is an agent or factor that provokes or speeds up a change or action without being consumed in the process itself. In the context of business or personal development, a catalyst can refer to a person, event, or idea that triggers significant progress, transformation, or innovation. Catalysts often facilitate positive change or growth by inspiring others, creating opportunities, or overcoming obstacles. They play a crucial role in driving forward momentum and sparking positive outcomes in various aspects of life or business.

6. Creativity:

Creativity is the ability to generate original ideas, solutions, or concepts that are novel, valuable, and relevant in a given context. It involves thinking outside the box, exploring new perspectives, and making connections between seemingly unrelated elements. Creativity encompasses a range of cognitive processes, including imagination, intuition, problem-solving, and divergent thinking. It manifests in various forms, such as artistic expression, innovation, design, and entrepreneurship. Creativity plays a crucial role in driving progress, driving innovation, and fostering individual and collective growth in diverse fields and industries.

7. Collaboration:

Collaboration is the process of individuals or groups working together to achieve a common goal or objective. It involves sharing ideas, resources, and responsibilities to generate solutions, make decisions, or complete tasks more effectively and efficiently than would be possible working alone. Collaboration often emphasizes communication, teamwork, and mutual respect among participants.

8. Conflict Resolution:

Conflict resolution refers to the process of addressing and resolving disagreements, disputes, or conflicts between individuals or groups in a constructive and peaceful manner. It involves identifying the underlying issues, understanding different perspectives, and finding mutually acceptable solutions that meet the needs and interests of all parties involved. Conflict resolution techniques may include negotiation, mediation, arbitration, compromise, or problem-solving strategies aimed at de-escalating tensions and fostering positive relationships.

9. COVID-19:

COVID-19, short for "Coronavirus Disease 2019," is a highly contagious respiratory illness caused by the novel coronavirus SARS-CoV-2. It was first identified in Wuhan, China, in December 2019 and has since spread globally, leading to a pandemic. COVID-19 primarily spreads through respiratory droplets when an infected person coughs, sneezes, or talks. Symptoms can range from mild to severe and may include fever, cough, shortness of breath, fatigue, muscle or body aches, loss of taste or smell, sore throat, congestion, nausea, or diarrhea. Severe cases can result in pneumonia, acute respiratory distress syndrome (ARDS), organ failure, and death. Various preventive measures, including vaccination, mask-wearing, hand hygiene, social distancing, and lockdowns, have been implemented worldwide to control the spread of the virus.

10. Coaching:

Coaching is a collaborative and goal-oriented process in which a coach works with an individual or a group to help them identify and achieve their personal or professional goals. Unlike traditional training, coaching focuses on empowering individuals to find their own solutions, make informed decisions, and maximize their potential. Coaches provide support, guidance, and feedback to facilitate self-discovery, skill development, and behavior change. Coaching sessions may cover various areas such as career development, leadership skills, personal growth, performance improvement, and overcoming challenges. The goal of coaching is to inspire and enable individuals to unlock their full potential, enhance their effectiveness, and achieve sustainable results.

D

11. Data-Based Decision-Making:

Data-based decision-making is an approach to decision-making that relies on the analysis of relevant data and information to inform choices and actions. Instead of relying solely on intuition or past experiences, organizations use data to identify trends, patterns, and insights that can guide decision-making processes. This approach involves collecting, analyzing, and interpreting data from various sources, such as surveys, market research, customer feedback, and operational metrics. By leveraging data, organizations can make more informed, objective, and evidence-based decisions, leading to improved outcomes and performance.

12. Dopamine:

Dopamine is a neurotransmitter, a chemical messenger in the brain that plays a crucial role in various functions, including movement, motivation, reward, and pleasure. It is involved in regulating mood, cognition, attention, learning, and the brain's pleasure and reward centers. Dopamine is also associated with addiction, as it contributes to feelings of pleasure and reinforcement, leading to the repetition of behaviors associated with its release.

13. Diversity & Inclusion:

Diversity and inclusion (D&I) refers to the collective mix of differences and similarities that exist among individuals within a particular organization or community, encompassing dimensions such as race, ethnicity, gender, age, sexual orientation, disability, socioeconomic background, religion, and cultural identity. Inclusive practices involve creating an environment where all individuals feel valued, respected, and empowered to contribute their unique perspectives and talents to the organization's goals and objectives. D&I initiatives aim to promote fairness, equity, and representation for all members of society, fostering innovation, collaboration, and organizational success.

E

14. Empathy:

Empathy is the ability to understand and share the feelings, thoughts, and perspectives of others. It involves being able to put oneself in someone else's shoes, to see things from their point of view, and to genuinely connect with their emotions and experiences. Empathy enables individuals to recognize and respond to the needs and concerns of others with compassion, kindness, and understanding. It is a fundamental aspect of emotional intelligence and interpersonal communication, fostering meaningful connections, support, and cooperation in personal and professional relationships.

15. Employee Engagement:

Employee engagement refers to the level of emotional commitment, motivation, and dedication that employees feel toward their work, organization, and goals. It encompasses factors such as job satisfaction, involvement in decision-making, alignment with organizational values, opportunities for growth and development, and the quality of relationships with colleagues and supervisors. Engaged employees are typically more productive, innovative, and loyal, leading to higher levels of performance, retention, and overall organizational success.

F

16. Fallibility:

Fallibility refers to the inherent tendency of human beings, systems, or processes to make mistakes, errors, or incorrect judgments. It acknowledges that no person or system is infallible and that errors are a natural part of human existence. Recognizing fallibility encourages humility, openness to feedback, and a willingness to learn from mistakes, ultimately fostering growth, improvement, and resilience in individuals and organizations.

G

17. Gen X:

Gen X, short for Generation X, refers to the demographic cohort born between the early to mid-1960s and the early 1980s, following the Baby Boomers and preceding the Millennials. Sometimes called the "Latchkey Generation," Gen Xers grew up during a time of significant societal changes, such as the rise of technology, the end of the Cold War, and shifting family structures. They are often characterized as independent, adaptable, and pragmatic, having navigated economic challenges and cultural shifts during their formative years. Gen Xers have made significant contributions to technology, pop culture, and the workforce, shaping the world in various ways.

18. Gen Z:

Gen Z, also known as Zoomers, is the demographic cohort succeeding Millennials and preceding Generation Alpha. Although the exact birth years defining Gen Z can vary slightly, it generally includes individuals born between the mid-1990s and the early 2010s. This generation has grown up in a digital age, with widespread access to technology and the internet from an early age. They are often characterized as tech-savvy, socially conscious, and diverse, with a strong emphasis on individual expression and inclusivity. Gen Zers are known for their fluency in digital communication, their entrepreneurial spirit, and their commitment to social justice and environmental sustainability.

H

19. HR Policy:

HR policy refers to a set of guidelines, rules, and procedures established by an organization to govern the management of its employees and their interactions within the workplace. These policies outline the organization's expectations, standards, and practices regarding various aspects of human resource management, including recruitment, hiring, compensation, benefits, performance evaluation, disciplinary procedures, and termination. HR policies aim to ensure consistency, fairness, compliance with legal requirements, and alignment with the organization's objectives and values. They provide clarity and guidance to employees and managers on acceptable behavior, rights, and responsibilities in the workplace.

I

20. Induction:

Induction, in the context of business or organizations, refers to the process of introducing newly hired employees to their roles, responsibilities, colleagues, and the overall work environment. It typically involves a structured program or orientation session designed to familiarize new employees with the company's policies, procedures, values, culture, and expectations. The purpose of induction is to help new employees integrate smoothly into their new roles, reduce the time it takes for them to become productive, and increase their job satisfaction and retention. Induction programs may include presentations, training sessions, meetings with key stakeholders, introductions to colleagues, tours of facilities, and the provision of necessary resources and tools to perform their jobs effectively.

J

21. Job Application:

A letter or form containing details of your qualifications, skills, experience, etc. that you send to an organization when you are applying for a job with them.

22. Job Interview:

Job interviews are structured conversations between a hiring manager or a panel of interviewers and a job applicant. The primary purpose of a job interview is for the employer to assess the applicant's qualifications, skills, experience, and suitability for the position. Job interviews typically involve a series of questions designed to evaluate the candidate's background, knowledge, competencies, and fit with the organization's culture and values. Interviews can take various formats, including face-to-face meetings, phone calls, video conferences, or group interviews.

K

23. Knowledge Transfer:

Knowledge transfer refers to the process of sharing information, skills, expertise, and insights from one individual or group to another within an organization or between organizations. It involves the transmission of knowledge from those who possess it (often termed "knowledge holders" or "subject matter experts") to those who need it to perform their roles effectively. Knowledge transfer can occur through various means, such as formal training programs, mentoring relationships, documentation, workshops, meetings, or informal discussions. The goal of knowledge transfer is to ensure that valuable knowledge is effectively disseminated throughout the organization, enabling individuals and teams to make informed decisions, solve problems, innovate, and improve performance. Effective knowledge transfer is essential for maintaining organizational continuity, fostering innovation, and supporting professional development.

L

24. Learning:

Learning refers to the acquisition of knowledge, skills, or understanding through study, experience, or teaching. It involves the process of absorbing new information and incorporating it into one's existing knowledge base.

25. Life Skills:

Life skills generally refer to a broader set of abilities that individuals use to navigate daily life and effectively handle various situations, challenges, and responsibilities. These skills encompass a wide range of competencies related to personal development, decision-making, problem-solving, and practical living. Examples of life skills include financial literacy, time management, decision-making, critical thinking, stress management, and resilience.

26. Lead through Action:

"Lead through action" refers to the practice of demonstrating leadership qualities and influencing others primarily through one's own behavior, decisions, and example. Instead of relying solely on words or directives, effective leaders lead by doing, embodying the values and principles they wish to instill in others. This approach often inspires trust, respect, and motivation among team members, fostering a culture of accountability, initiative, and continuous improvement within the organization.

M

27. Mentor:

A mentor is an experienced and trusted advisor who provides guidance, support, and encouragement to a less experienced individual, known as a mentee or protégé. Mentors typically possess expertise, knowledge, and skills in a particular field or domain and willingly share their insights and experiences to help the mentee develop professionally and personally. They offer valuable advice, share resources, constructive feedback, and serve as role models for their mentees. Mentoring relationships are often built on mutual respect, trust, and confidentiality, and they can be formal or informal arrangements within organizations or professional networks. The primary goal of mentoring is to foster the mentee's growth, learning, and development, ultimately enabling them to reach their full potential and achieve their goals.

28. Manager:

A manager is an individual within an organization who is responsible for overseeing and coordinating the activities of a team or department to achieve organizational goals and objectives. Managers typically have authority over a group of employees and are accountable for planning, organizing, directing, and controlling the resources and processes necessary to accomplish specific tasks or projects. They play a key role in decision-making, setting priorities, allocating resources, managing budgets, resolving conflicts, and evaluating performance. Managers often possess strong leadership, communication, and interpersonal skills, as well as expertise in their area of responsibility. Their primary focus is on achieving results, fostering teamwork, and driving continuous improvement within their team or department.

29. Machine Learning:

Machine Learning is a subset of Artificial Intelligence (AI) that involves the development of algorithms and statistical models that enable computers to perform tasks without being explicitly programmed for them. Compared to AI, machine learning algorithms learn from and make predictions or decisions based on data. These algorithms iteratively learn from data, identify patterns, and make decisions or predictions, improving over time with more data and feedback. Machine learning is used in various applications, including predictive analytics, natural language processing, image recognition, and recommendation systems.

N

30. Negotiation:

Negotiation in communication refers to the interactive process through which parties involved in a discussion or transaction seek to reach a mutually acceptable agreement or resolution to a conflict or issue. Effective negotiation involves active listening, clear articulation of interests and goals, understanding of the other party's perspective, and the ability to explore and generate creative solutions that satisfy both parties' needs. It often requires empathy, flexibility, assertiveness, and strategic thinking to navigate differences and find common ground while preserving relationships and achieving desired outcomes.

O

31. Oxytocin:

Oxytocin is a hormone and neurotransmitter often referred to as the "love hormone" or "bonding hormone" because of its role in social bonding, childbirth, and breastfeeding. It is produced in the hypothalamus and released by the pituitary gland. Oxytocin plays a crucial role in facilitating childbirth by stimulating uterine contractions and promoting milk ejection during breastfeeding. Additionally, it is involved in promoting social bonding, trust, empathy, and maternal behavior. Oxytocin has also been linked to various physiological and psychological effects, including reducing stress and anxiety, increasing feelings of contentment and relaxation, and enhancing social interactions.

P

32. PoSH:

PoSH stands for Prevention of Sexual Harassment, which refers to a set of laws, guidelines, and measures implemented by organizations and governments to prevent and address instances of sexual harassment in the workplace. PoSH policies typically include procedures for reporting incidents of sexual harassment, conducting investigations, and providing support to victims. These policies aim to create a safe and respectful work environment for all employees, free from any form of harassment or discrimination based on gender or sex. Compliance with PoSH regulations is essential for organizations to promote gender equality, protect employee rights, and maintain a positive workplace culture.

33. Performance Appraisal:

Performance appraisal, also known as performance review or evaluation, is a systematic process used by organizations to assess and evaluate the job performance of employees. It involves measuring employees' achievements, strengths, weaknesses, and areas for improvement against predetermined goals, job responsibilities, and performance standards. Performance appraisals typically occur on a regular basis, such as annually or biannually, and involve feedback sessions between employees and their supervisors or managers. The purpose of performance appraisal is to provide employees with constructive feedback, recognize their contributions, identify areas for development, set new goals, and make decisions related to promotions, compensation, training, and career advancement. It also serves as a basis for performance-based rewards, performance management, and organizational planning.

R

34. Relearning:

Relearning is the process of acquiring new knowledge or skills that were previously learned but may have been forgotten or become obsolete. It involves refreshing or updating one's understanding of a subject or concept that was previously known but has changed over time.

35. Reskilling:

Reskilling refers to the process of learning new skills or updating existing ones to adapt to changes in job roles, industry trends, or technological advancements. It involves acquiring additional knowledge and competencies that may be different from one's current skill set in order to remain relevant and competitive in the workforce. Reskilling initiatives are often undertaken to address skill gaps, meet evolving job requirements, or transition to new career opportunities. The goal of reskilling is to enhance employability, career advancement, and professional growth by acquiring the necessary skills and expertise demanded by the changing landscape of work.

S

36. SMART Goals:

SMART goals are a framework for setting objectives that are Specific, Measurable, Achievable, Relevant, and Time-bound. This acronym helps ensure that goals are clear, quantifiable, realistic, aligned with organizational objectives, and have a defined timeframe for completion. By setting SMART goals, individuals and organizations can increase their chances of success by providing clarity, focus, and accountability.

37. Soft Skills:

Soft skills specifically focus on interpersonal and social abilities that enable individuals to interact effectively with others in personal, professional, and social settings. Soft skills are often related to communication, collaboration, emotional intelligence, and interpersonal relationships.

38. Skilling:

Skilling refers to the process of developing specific skills or competencies necessary for performing a particular job or task effectively. It involves acquiring both technical and non-technical abilities through training, education, and practical experience. Skilling initiatives are aimed at equipping individuals with the knowledge and capabilities required to excel in their chosen profession or field of work. Skilling programs may focus on various areas such as technical skills, soft skills, leadership skills, communication skills, and problem-solving abilities, depending on the specific needs of the job or industry. The goal of skilling is to enhance employability, productivity, and overall performance in the workplace.

39. Sharpen the Axe:

In corporate terms, "sharpen the axe" refers to the proactive process of investing in continuous learning, skill development and strategic planning to enhance organizational effectiveness and achieve long-term success. Just as a well-maintained tool can accomplish tasks more efficiently, organizations that prioritize training, innovation, and adaptation can improve their competitive edge, productivity, and ability to navigate challenges in the ever-evolving business landscape. This approach emphasizes the importance of proactive preparation, ongoing improvement, and staying ahead of the curve to achieve sustainable growth and excellence in the corporate world.

T

40. Technical Skills:

Technical skills are specific abilities and knowledge required to perform tasks related to a particular field, industry, or profession. These skills are typically practical, job-specific competencies that enable individuals to effectively execute tasks, solve problems, and achieve objectives within their area of expertise. Technical skills can vary widely depending on the profession or industry but may include proficiency in using software, operating machinery, performing scientific experiments, conducting data analysis, programming, engineering, or any other specialized skill set relevant to the individual's job or field of study.

41. Training:

Training refers to the process of imparting knowledge, skills, and competencies to individuals or groups in order to enhance their performance, productivity, and effectiveness in a particular area or job role. It involves structured instruction, learning activities, and practical exercises designed to develop specific abilities and improve job-related performance. Training programs can cover a wide range of topics, including technical skills, soft skills, professional development, compliance training, safety procedures, and more. The ultimate goal of training is to empower individuals with the knowledge and capabilities they need to excel in their roles and contribute to the success of their organization.

42. Thinking outside the box:

"Thinking outside the box" refers to the ability to approach problems, tasks, or situations in unconventional or innovative ways, often by breaking away from traditional or conventional thinking patterns. This mindset encourages creativity, originality, and exploration of new perspectives or solutions that may not be immediately obvious. By challenging assumptions, exploring diverse viewpoints, and embracing experimentation, individuals or organizations can uncover fresh insights and breakthrough ideas that lead to greater innovation and success.

U

43. Unlearning:

Unlearning involves letting go of outdated or incorrect beliefs, assumptions, or behaviors. It requires actively challenging and discarding previously held notions that may no longer be relevant or accurate.

44. Upskilling:

Upskilling refers to the process of acquiring new knowledge, skills, or competencies to enhance one's abilities in a particular field or profession. It involves actively seeking out opportunities for learning and development to stay relevant in a rapidly changing job market or industry. Upskilling may involve formal education, training programs, workshops, certifications, or self-directed learning initiatives aimed at improving existing skills or acquiring new ones. The goal of upskilling is to increase an individual's value and competitiveness in the workforce, leading to improved job performance, career advancement, and opportunities for personal growth.

-------------------- The Beginning --------------------

**Transforming Minds, Empowering Futures:
Discover the Artful Approach to HR Concepts.**

Hi readers,

I am Dr. V. Vijay Anand Sriram. With a wealth of experience spanning over two decades, I've traversed various domains as the Co-founder and CEO of RIPE Consulting Services Pvt Ltd and the Chief Strategist of CogEds Technologies Pvt Ltd. My journey has been marked by a relentless pursuit of knowledge and excellence, reflected in my extensive academic background comprising over 8 degrees and completion of more than 20 certificate courses.

Throughout my career, I've been deeply involved in personal and business development, excelling in human resource management & development, soft skills, psychology, strategic management, and business consulting. My doctoral research venture, "Ancient Wisdom and Modern Management Principles," undertaken over 8 years, underscores my dedication to addressing contemporary HR challenges through rigorous research and insightful synthesis.

As a global trainer and motivational speaker, I've had the privilege of impacting a vast audience worldwide through transformative talks and seminars, reaching countless individuals through numerous events. My expertise has benefited over 100 prestigious companies and 500 educational institutions, focusing on vital areas such as leadership, communication, strategy, creativity, and success psychology.

In addition to my professional endeavors, I am an accomplished author and filmmaker, known for my best-selling book, "Oru Siragu Podhum," Vikatan Publications and for directing the thought-provoking movie- "AAGAM." My influence extends to core research contributions for notable films such as Thani Oruvan, Velaikaran, and Godfather (Telugu), along with appearances in 100 + TV shows and numerous articles in respected publications.

My latest endeavor, "Artful Approach," encapsulates my two decades of experience in HR concepts, offering innovative solutions and strategies presented poetically. This book delves into the transformative power of poetry in addressing HR challenges, providing readers with a unique and insightful perspective on the subject.

Beyond my professional pursuits, I am the founder-president of the "TATTVAMASI" Educational Charitable Trust, committed to philanthropic activities. As a loving husband and father, I embody a holistic approach to life, continually striving to inspire and empower those around me.

With Love

Dr. V. VIJAY ANAND SRIRAM

**B.Sc (Hons), MBA (Gold Medal),
PGDHRM, PGDHR, PGDHRD,
MS, EPSM (IIM K), PhD**